TERRIFIC TRANSPORTATION INVENTIONS

LAURA HAMILTON WAXMAN

LERNER PUBLICATIONS COMPANY
MINNEAPOLIS

Lerner Publications Company
A division of Lerner Publishing Group, Inc.
241 First Avenue North
Minneapolis, MN 55401 U.S.A.

Website address: www.lernerbooks.com

Library of Congress Cataloging-in-Publication Data

Waxman, Laura Hamilton.
Terrific transportation inventions /
by Laura Hamilton Waxman.
p.   cm. — (Awesome inventions you use every day)
Summary: "A fun "grab–bag" of off–the–wall factoids
introduces readers to awesome inventions related to
transportation and vehicles"–Provided by publisher.
Includes index.
ISBN 978–1–4677–1096–1 (lib. bdg. : alk. paper)
ISBN 978–1–4677–1688–8 (eBook)
1. Transportation—Juvenile literature. 2. Automobiles—
Juvenile literature. 3. Airplanes—Juvenile literature.
4. Passenger trains—Juvenile literature. 5. Passenger
ships—Juvenile literature. 6. Space shuttles—
Juvenile literature. I. Title.
TA1149.W38 2014
629.04′6—dc23   2012046912

Manufactured in the United States of America
1 – BP – 7/15/13

CONTENTS

INTRODUCTION

GOING SOMEWHERE FAST

How do you get around? Do you hitch a ride in a parent's car? Pedal on a bike? Take the train or the bus? These days, getting around usually involves some sort of vehicle. We're a speedy bunch, after all. We expect to get places fast.

That wasn't true thousands of years ago. In ancient times, you'd probably travel by foot or maybe on horseback. That's how you'd hunt for food, visit neighboring communities, settle in new lands, and do just about everything else. Hundreds of years later, after the wheel was invented, you might ride in a carriage or a wagon. But mostly you'd rely on your own two feet, like those ancestors long ago. Kids your age walked to school, and their parents walked to town every now and then to get supplies. If someone back then said he wanted to invent a horseless vehicle to get from point A to point B? That'd be crazy talk!

That's what makes the story of transportation so amazing. It took some smart, determined, and inventive people to say, "No, it's *not* crazy. And I'll prove it." Someone had to build the first motorized car. Someone had to dream up the first submarine. And someone had to design the first passenger airplane. To read about these surprising, wacky, and inspiring stories, turn the page!

4

In years past, most people used horses to travel long distances.

In modern times, people have lots of transportation choices. Most big cities have passenger trains like this one.

PASSENGER SHIP

What if you could invent a machine powered by hot air? Would you do it? If you were American inventor Robert Fulton, you'd say, "Heck yeah!" In the early 1800s, he found a way to harness the power of steam to make a ship that could move way faster than most other ships at the time. And his invention set the stage for traveling across the world's oceans in style.

Before airplanes, people traveled the globe on sailing ships. For hundreds of years, that meant relying on a good, stiff breeze to fill the sails and move the boat. But the wind could only push a ship so fast. And if there was no wind? That meant no go.

In 1807 Fulton designed the first successful boat powered by a steam engine. Over time, other inventors improved on his idea. By the mid-1800s, steamships were up to two-thirds faster than other ships. The first steamships were probably windy, wet, and miserable. Most passengers rode in the open and were exposed to the wind and rain. So companies began to build oceangoing ships with comfortable rooms, electric lights, and other luxuries. In these passenger ships, people traveled in style.

By the early 1900s, passenger ships looked like enormous floating hotels. They offered passengers entertaining activities such as dancing and elegant dining. Riding on a passenger ship was a fun and fancy vacation. (Unless you were on the 1912 *Titanic* voyage. When that ship hit an iceberg and sank, it wasn't fun *or* fancy.)

By the 1960s, airplanes were taking over the skies. Fewer people traveled by sea. But the passenger ship biz didn't go under. It transformed into the modern cruise ship industry. These days, millions of people all around the world still love to say *Bon Voyage*! (That's French for "Have a great trip!")

PASSENGER AIRPLANE

These days, it's no biggie to look up and see a passenger airplane overhead. But in the early days of flight, airplanes weren't practical—or affordable for most people. Inside the planes, passengers braved ear-blasting noise from the engines. Not to mention that airplanes weren't as safe as they are in modern times. Passengers were at a serious risk of getting hurt or losing their lives in a crash.

A company called Transcontinental World Airlines (TWA) set out to change that. In 1932 it hooked up with airplane expert Donald Douglas. Douglas designed the first passenger plane. His twelve-seat DC-1 had heaters, soundproofing, and automatic pilot. Even so, most Americans weren't impressed. They said, "Thanks but no thanks."

Then Douglas came out with his twin-engine DC-3 in 1936. It carried a whopping twenty-one passengers and could be flown nonstop from New York to Chicago. That might not seem like a big deal to you. But back then? It was huge. Passenger airplanes allowed more people to travel farther and faster than ever before. By 1960 planes were transporting 62 million Americans each year.

That wasn't nearly enough for Juan Trippe and William Allen. Trippe owned the passenger airline Pan Am. Allen was the president of plane manufacturer Boeing. Together, these two guys oversaw the creation of a monster plane. The Boeing 747 came out in 1968. It was an epic 225 feet (68 meters) long. Its total wing area was bigger than a basketball court. And it held 374 passengers and their luggage. The 747 took the passenger airplane to a whole new level. Other big planes followed. By the 2000s, more than 600 million Americans were flying on passenger planes each year.

BICYCLE

Buses and cars run on gasoline. But bikes? They run on human energy: your own pedal power!

For most of history, people relied on riding animals to get from points A to B. Or they rode inside carts pulled by oxen or horses. A human-powered vehicle was just a crazy dream. Then German Karl von Drais invented a vehicle that didn't require a horse in 1817. Instead of four legs and hooves, von Drais's vehicle relied on two wooden wheels and two human feet. Too bad he forgot the pedals. He had to move his two-wheeler by pushing his feet off the ground.

Fifty years later, Frenchman Pierre Michaux introduced another two-wheeler. But this one had pedals. It also had a stiff frame and hard metal and wood wheels. The ride was so rough that it soon earned the nickname the bone shaker.

Bone shakers weren't just uncomfortable. They didn't go very fast either. To solve that problem, other bicycle makers built bicycles with big front wheels. The larger the wheel, the faster the bike moved. And the farther the rider could fall. Ouch!

Was a fast *and* safe bike too much to ask? Not if you were British bicycle maker J. K. Starley. He introduced his "safety bike" in 1885. It had two wheels, both the same smaller size. And it was speedy. A chain attached to the back wheel made all the difference. The pedals moved the chain, which helped the bike gain speed. After that, bikes really took off. Kids have been doing wheelies ever since.

CAN YOU IMAGINE YOUR MOM, DAD, OR GRANDMA RIDING A GIANT TRICYCLE? If they had lived in the 1870s, they just might have. The first tricycles were made for grown-ups, not kids. They were a safer choice than those dangerous high wheelers.

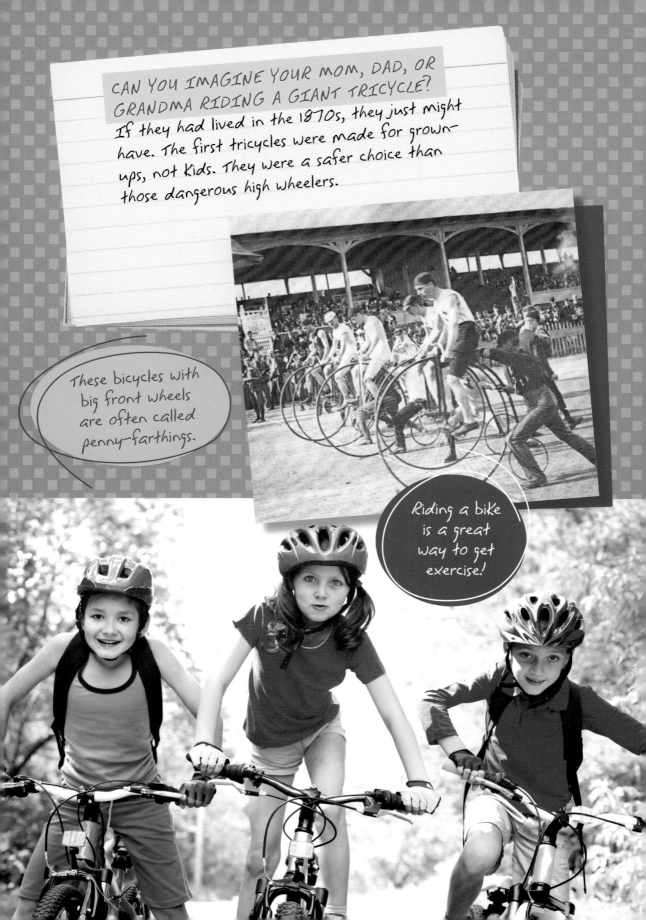

These bicycles with big front wheels are often called penny-farthings.

Riding a bike is a great way to get exercise!

TRACTOR

Before tractors, farmers used strong animals such as oxen, mules, or horses to pull plows and other farm equipment. And if they didn't own farm animals? They strapped the equipment to their own bodies.

Steam engines became widely available in the early to mid-1800s, and so did better solutions for farmers. For example, in 1875 the C. & G. Cooper Company invented the first steam-powered tractor. It was supposed to replace farm animals altogether. But it was missing one thing: a steering wheel. Farmers had to hitch a team of horses to the tractor to keep it going in a straight line. Once Cooper added a steering wheel, tractor sales got a whole lot better.

Even so, most farmers stayed away from steam-powered tractors. They were expensive to buy. And they were a pain to fuel. No one wanted to keep stopping to stuff wood, coal, or straw into the engine. Iowa businessman John Froelich had a better idea. In 1892 he invented the first gas-powered tractor. Gas engines didn't need to be refueled as often as steam-powered ones. And unlike earlier tractors, his machine could move either forward or backward.

Little by little, tractors replaced horses and other working farm animals. In the 1920s, U.S. companies were making more than twenty thousand tractors each year. By the mid-1900s, almost four million tractors were hard at work on American farms. Tractors were here to stay. (And tired farm animals across the nation rejoiced.) In the twenty-first century, modern farmers ride in air-conditioned tractors with digital displays.

MANY AMERICANS THINK OF JOHN DEERE WHEN THEY THINK OF TRACTORS. But John Deere actually made his living selling steel plows. His company, John Deere (named for himself, of course), didn't make its first tractor until 1918. That was thirty-two years after Deere died.

A man uses a horse to plow his field in the 1930s.

Modern tractors are comfortable and full of high-tech gadgets.

SUBMARINE

Did you know that the world's first underwater boat had to be rowed by twelve men? Twelve very brave men.

This early submarine was the brainchild of Cornelis Drebbel. He worked as a royal inventor for King James I of England in the 1600s. In 1615 Drebbel made a vessel out of wood. Then he wrapped it in leather and smeared it with grease to make sure water couldn't seep in. The boat made at least one successful trip beneath the surface of the Thames River in London. But people weren't exactly lining up for a ride. (Would *you* want to travel underwater without a source of fresh air?)

Then came the American Revolutionary War (1775–1783). The American forces needed a way to make big British ships go *kaboom*! They wondered if an underwater boat could plant explosives on enemy vessels. In 1775 American David Bushnell built a small submarine from iron and wood. He called it the *Turtle*, but it looked more like a giant walnut. The underwater walnut was no match for British warships, though. It failed miserably at attaching explosives to enemy ships.

During the American Civil War (1861–1865), subs got another try. Horace Hunley designed an iron sub for the Southern navy. A modest guy, Hunley named the sub after himself. In test runs, the H. L. *Hunley* sank three times. (The second time, its inventor was inside it and died.) The Southern navy used Hunley's sub anyway, and it sank an enormous Northern ship, the *Housatonic*. This victory proved that subs were worth keeping around.

Eleven years later, an Irish American named John P. Holland invented the first gasoline-powered sub. That revolutionary idea inspired the modern submarine, which is powered by nuclear energy.

This sketch shows the H. L. Hunley.

One of the U.S. Navy's nuclear submarines returns to its naval base.

CAR

Imagine a world without paved streets, traffic jams, or road rage. Imagine roads full of carriages and horse poop. Imagine taking all day to travel 30 miles (48 kilometers). You have just imagined life before the car.

Humans lived in a car-free zone for thousands of years. Then came gas-powered engines in the 1860s and the 1870s. That set off a race to invent the first gas-powered automobile.

It came down to two Germans, Karl Benz and Gottlieb Daimler. The men didn't know each other. But they shared the same dream. Benz got there first in 1886. He called his three-wheeled car the Motorwagen. Sure, it looked like a carriage stuck on a big tricycle. But who cared? It worked! Soon after, Daimler built the world's second successful gas car. Meanwhile, other car companies started popping up all over the place. So did car-buying customers. Over time, cars went from giant tricycles to powerful four-wheelers.

By the 1940s, cars had been crowned kings of the road. And in 2012, about 60 million cars were built around the world. Now that's a lot of cars!

The Motorwagen looked more like a big tricycle than a modern car.

SMASH! BANG! BOOM! Without traffic lights, that's what you'd hear all the time. The world's first traffic light appeared in London in 1868. Its job was to control carriage traffic at night. Unfortunately, the thing exploded one day and killed a police officer. The idea of traffic lights died with him.

Then cars came along and brought chaos with them. Without traffic lights, cars were crashing into carriages, bikes, and one another. The first city to come to its senses was Cleveland, Ohio. It set up green and red traffic lights in 1914. Four years later, New York City added a third color, yellow.

MOTORCYCLE

People in the early 1800s loved getting around quickly on bicycles. But it still wasn't fast enough for some. What to do? For a couple of courageous guys, the answer was to add an engine.

One of those guys was American speed lover Sylvester H. Roper. In the 1860s, he figured out how to build a steam-powered bicycle. It had a wooden frame and a large steam engine. Roper's motorbike was fun to ride. But it got him arrested for being a speed demon!

People paid twenty-five cents to watch Roper ride his two-wheeled beast. No one else was brave enough to try it out, though. Good call. Roper met his end while riding his whizzing machine.

In Germany Gottlieb Daimler was working on motorcycles too. He invented the first gas-powered motorcycle in 1885. Like Roper, Daimler attached an engine to a wooden bicycle frame. *Unlike* Roper he wasn't crazy enough to test it himself. He made his son Paul do it instead.

The motorcycle industry took off. Soon motorcycle frames were being made of metal, not wood. And instead of wooden wheels, motorcycles had air-filled rubber tires for a smoother ride. By the early 1900s, Americans had lost their fear of motorcycles. That's when the modern motorcycle really got into gear. Motorcycles—and the adventurous people who ride them—have been around ever since.

THE HARLEY-DAVIDSON MOTOR COMPANY is one of the biggest motorcycle makers in the world. The company started in Milwaukee, Wisconsin, in 1903. William S. Harley and Arthur Davidson made their first motorcycle in a 10-×-15-foot (3×4.6 m) wooden shed. In 2013 Harley-Davidson produced more than 250,000 motorcycles.
Vroom-vroom!

Daimler's 1885 motorcycle (BELOW) wasn't comfortable or safe to drive.

SEMITRUCK

Some inventions are sparked by a simple question. That's true of the eighteen-wheel semitruck. It all started with August Charles Fruehauf, a blacksmith and a carriage maker. Fruehauf was living in Detroit, Michigan, in the early 1900s. One day a buddy came to him with a problem. The friend needed a better way to transport his heavy sailboat to the lake. Could Fruehauf make it happen?

No problem, said Fruehauf. He got right to work and—ta-da! Fruehauf built a semitrailer—a platform with wheels underneath. His friend then attached the trailer to his car. Why did Fruehauf call his invention a semitrailer? Probably because *semi* means "half." Fruehauf's trailer had only two wheels (at the back), half of the wheels on a truck or car.

The semitrailer was just the thing Fruehauf's friend needed. He wasn't the only one. Soon other folks were lining up for semitrailers of their own.

Fruehauf's trailer business had taken off. But he wasn't finished. In 1916 he came up with the tractor-trailer. This vehicle was a truck with an enclosed cab for the driver.

Together, the truck and the semitrailer formed a semitruck. At first, the semitruck was mostly used in the military. During World War I (1914–1918), the U.S. Army ordered thousands of them to haul supplies. But after the war, people began using semitrucks for other things too. In the twenty-first century, trucks transport everything from the food you eat and the clothes you wear to giant road-building machines and more. Fruehauf would be proud.

This semitruck was on the road in the 1930s.

Semitrucks are a common sight on roads and highways in the United States.

SPACE SHUTTLE

Before space shuttles were invented, astronauts flew into outer space in space capsules. These metal cones were shot into space like bullets. Upon their return, they fell through Earth's atmosphere at neck-breaking speeds. The ride back to Earth ended with a splash landing in the ocean. The space capsule was then laid to rest.

There had to be a better way.

In the 1970s, engineers at the National Aeronautics and Space Administration (NASA) got to work on a new kind of spacecraft. Their goal? To invent a reusable flying machine that was also safer.

What they came up with was a spacecraft modeled after the airplane. NASA named this first space shuttle the *Columbia*. It had a huge orange fuel tank and two rocket boosters that fell away as the shuttle launched into space. An orbiter (the part that looks like a plane) carried the crew. The orbiter also had three engines of its own. This allowed the pilots to land the craft like an airplane. No more crashing into oceans.

NASA launched *Columbia* for the first time in 1981. Over the years, NASA built four other space shuttles. Together, these shuttles launched more than 130 times. They carried more than 350 people into space. And they traveled a total of 500 million miles (804.7 million km). Talk about a spacy road trip!

NASA ended its thirty-year space shuttle program in 2011. For now, it's back to space capsules for astronauts traveling to outer space. But private companies are working on shuttles of their own. Someday, a space shuttle could take *you* into orbit.

A space capsule splashes down in the Pacific Ocean in 1971.

THE SPACE SHUTTLES AREN'T FLYING ANYMORE.
But they're not sitting on blocks in NASA's garage either. Four shuttle orbiters are on public display at science and space centers around the country. How'd the orbiters get to their new homes? They took turns getting a piggyback ride on a special jumbo jet.

Space shuttle *Atlantis* lands at Kennedy Space Center in Florida in 2009.

BUS

Did you know that in the 1800s, there was no such thing as a bus? Most people hitched rides in carriages pulled by horses. That all changed when a young British science geek got buses rolling in the early 1800s.

Walter Hancock was fascinated by the steam engine—a new invention at the time. He used it to invent the world's first engine-powered buses. He called his biggest bus the *Automaton*. It seated twenty-two passengers. And it traveled through London, England, at a speedy 22 miles (35 km) per hour. Hancock's customers loved it. But the guys who drove horse-and-carriage vehicles? Not so much. They worried that buses such as Hancock's would take over the city and put them out of business. So they helped pass new city rules to force him—and his buses—off the road.

By the end of the century, gas-powered cars were on the way in. That really put carriages out of business! And it led to the first gas-powered bus, which was built in England in 1899. In the 1900s, buses replaced horse-drawn carriages for good.

This illustration shows Walter Hancock's steam-powered bus, the Enterprise.

EVER WONDER WHY SCHOOL BUSES ARE ALL PAINTED YELLOW? Why not blue or pink or even polka-dotted? Before the 1940s, buses did come in all colors, sizes, and shapes. One city painted its buses a patriotic red, white, and blue.

All those colors seemed unsafe to education professor Frank W. Cyr. So in 1939, he got school officials, bus manufacturers, and paint companies together. They designed the yellow school bus. Why yellow? The black letters that spell out "School Bus" stand out the best against a yellow background. So the next time you see a bright yellow bus, think of Professor Cyr.

SCHOOL

PASSENGER TRAIN

Railways were around long before passenger trains. But you'd have to be a piece of coal or iron to ride the first railways. And you'd be pulled by a horse, not an engine. The first engine-powered train was designed by British inventor Richard Trevithick in 1804. It did a great job of carrying lumps of iron at 5 miles (8 km) per hour. But it didn't do much to help the carriage-riding public.

British businessman George Stephenson set out to get people onto trains. In 1830 he opened the first passenger railway. It stretched 30 miles (48 km) between Liverpool and Manchester in England. Stephenson's son, Robert, designed the railway's train. He called it the *Rocket* because it was so speedy. The *Rocket* could go as fast as 29 miles (46 km) per hour. Sounds slow, right? But at that time, most people were traveling by horse and buggy. Absolutely no horse could run that fast for that long.

Pretty soon, folks started choosing to go by train instead of by carriage. In the United States, more tracks for passenger trains were built between towns and cities. About 30,000 miles (48,280 km) of track were built in just thirty years.

Automobiles took over U.S. roads in the 1940s, so Americans didn't take trains as much anymore. But in some parts of the country, Americans still take the train. For example, if you want to go from Boston to Washington, D.C., you can take the Acela Express. It goes as fast as 150 miles (240 km) per hour.

TRAINS HAVE COME A LONG WAY SINCE STEPHENSON'S ROCKET. Modern high-speed trains are called bullet trains for a reason. These sleek babies shoot over the rails at crazy-high speeds. Bullet trains travel up to 250 miles (402 km) per hour. The world's fastest bullet train is in China. It zooms along the tracks at speeds up to 268 miles (431 km) per hour.

Curious passersby check out the *Rocket*.

A bullet train runs on an elevated track in Kyoto, Japan.

HELICOPTER

Airplanes are great for flying long distances. But can they hover in the air? Can they fly backward and sideways? And can they take off and land from a standstill position? Nope. The only vehicle that can do all that is the helicopter. *Thwack-thwack-thwack!*

The first helicopters were invented in the early 1900s. But they could barely get off the ground. They shook violently. They were almost impossible to balance and steer. And they had a nasty habit of crashing and burning.

Then Igor Sikorsky came along. This Russian American inventor owned his own aircraft company. Like other inventors, he'd tried and failed to design a helicopter. Then inspiration struck. Why not use two propellers—one for power and the other for balance? The balancing propeller, or rotor, was attached to the helicopter's metal tail. The power propeller was attached on top.

It was a good idea. But like many ideas, it needed a lot of fiddling to work. All that fussing drove Sikorsky's workers crazy. They started calling his tailed helicopter Igor's nightmare. But by 1940, Sikorsky had perfected his invention. It became the model for all future helicopters.

Igor Sikorsky hovers in a helicopter in the 1940s.

HELICOPTERS BECAME REALLY POPULAR IN THE 1960S AS A MILITARY VEHICLE. They were used for everything from rescuing wounded U.S. soldiers on the battlefield to flying on spy missions. Since then, they've been put to use for lots of other cool jobs. Firefighters put out wildfires, medics rush patients to hospitals, and police follow high-speed car chases—all from helicopters. They've even been used to track down zoo animals on the loose.

This modern military helicopter is called a Sikorsky UH-60 Black Hawk.

GLOSSARY

American Civil War: the war between the Northern and Southern states. It started in April 1861, and the North won the war in 1865.

American Revolutionary War: the war for U.S. independence between the American colonists and the British. The war lasted from 1775 to 1783.

atmosphere: the layer of gases surrounding a planet

bullet train: a high-speed passenger train

carriage: a vehicle with at least four wheels that is pulled by horses

jet: an airplane powered by jet engines that run on aviation fuel. These engines use the force of air to thrust the aircraft forward.

orbiter: the part of a space shuttle where crew members sit and work

plow: a heavy farming tool pulled by a tractor or a farm animal. Plows break up soil and make narrow trenches with their sharp blades.

propeller: spinning blades that move a helicopter through the air

rotor: the propeller on a helicopter that helps balance the vehicle in the air

semitrailer: a trailer that attaches to the back of a truck

space capsule: a cone-shaped spacecraft that transports people into outer space

steam engine: an engine that runs on steam

FURTHER INFORMATION

America on the Move
    http://www.americanhistory.si.edu/onthemove
    Visit this website to learn more about the history of transportation.
    You can play a game or two while you're there.

Bortz, Fred. *Seven Wonders of Exploration Technology*. Minneapolis:
    Twenty-First Century Books, 2010. This book takes you on
    an exploration of outer space and the deep seas—and the
    transportation inventions that make such exploration possible.

FAA: Kids Corner
    http://www.faa.gov/education/student_resources/kids_corner
    /ages_10_12
    Check out this website from the Federal Aviation Administration
    for information about flight.

Fridell, Ron. *Seven Wonders of Transportation*. Minneapolis: Twenty-
    First Century Books, 2010. Read this book to learn more about
    vehicles that changed the world.

Herbst, Judith. *The History of Transportation*. Minneapolis: Lerner
    Publications Company, 2006. Discover the fascinating history,
    inventions, and development of human transportation.

Inventors and Inventions
    http://www.kidskonnect.com/subject-index/15-science/86-
    inventors-a-inventions.html
    This kid-friendly site is loaded with information links related
    to inventions and inventors.

Kassoy, Ben, and Michael J. Rosen. *Bizarre Vehicles*. Minneapolis:
    Millbrook Press, 2014. Read about strange and fascinating
    forms of transportation in this fun book.

Woods, Michael, and Mary B. Woods. *Ancient Transportation
    Technology: From Oars to Elephants*. Minneapolis: Twenty-
    First Century Books, 2011. This book explores the history of
    transportation in ancient cultures.

INDEX

PHOTO ACKNOWLEDGMENTS

The images in this book are used with the permission of: The Granger Collection, New York, pp. 5 (top), 19 (bottom); © Tim Macpherson/Stone/Getty Images, p. 5 (bottom); Library of Congress pp. 7 (top LC-USZ62-20997); 12 (middle LC-USF33-T01-002407-M2); © Bettmann/CORBIS, pp. 7 (middle), 17 (top); © Brett Critchley/Dreamstime.com, p. 7 (bottom); © iStockphoto/Thinkstock, p. 9 (top); © Charles Fenno Jacobs/Time Life Pictures/Getty Images, p. 9 (middle); © PhotoAlto/Thierry Foulon/Getty Images, p. 9 (bottom); © iStockphoto.com/wdstock, pp. 11 (top), 13 (top), 19 (top), 23 (middle), 27 (top), 29 (middle); © Hulton-Deutsch Collection/CORBIS, p. 11 (middle); © Dmitriy Shironosov/Dreamstime.com, p. 11 (bottom); © Soleg1974/Dreamstime.com, p. 13 (bottom); U.S. Naval Institute Heritage Collection, p. 15 (top); U.S. Navy photo by Mass Communication Specialist 1st Class James Kimber/Released, p. 15 (bottom); © Andreus/Dreamstime.com, p. 15 (inset); © iStockphoto.com/Nicholas Belton, pp. 17 (bottom), 25 (middle); © Tyler Olson/Dreamstime.com, p. 17 (inset right); © iStockphoto.com/Henrick Jonsson, p. 17 (inset left); © Goncaloferreira/Dreamstime.com, p. 19; Lee Brothers, Minnesota Historical Society, p. 21 (top); © Jgroup/Dreamstime.com, p. 21 (bottom); © NASA/Time Life Pictures/Getty Images, p. 23 (top); NASA , p. 23 (bottom); Ziskqs/Wikimedia Commons, p. 25 (top); © Keith Brofsky/UpperCut Images/Getty Images, p. 25 (bottom); © Mary Evans Picture Library/Alamy, p. 27 (middle); © Naoto Shibata/Flickr/Getty Images, p. 27 (bottom); U.S Coast Guard/Wikimedia Commons, p. 29 (top); © iStockphoto.com/Dieter Spears, p. 29 (bottom).
Front cover: © iStockphoto.com/Baris Simsek.

Main body text set in Highlander ITC Std Book 13/16. Typeface provided by International Typeface Corp.